MADE NEW

Healing and Hope for Abuse Survivors

Crystalina & Jason Evert

Totus Tuus
PRESS

2019

Made New: Healing and Hope for Abuse Survivors
Crystalina & Jason Evert
© 2019 Totus Tuus Press, LLC.

Published by Totus Tuus Press, LLC.
P.O. Box 5065
Scottsdale, AZ 85261
www.totustuuspress.com

Cover by Devin Schadt
Interior by Russell Graphic Design

Printed in the United States of America

978-1-944578-88-6
978-1-944578-89-3 eBook

Foreword

Crystalina once said to me:

"Jason, do you want to know a little secret about women? We are masters at stuffing our stuff. When bad stuff happens in our lives, we just stuff it. On the outside, everything looks put together; our hair looks great and our makeup is flawless. But inside we feel like a tangled mess. So we numb ourselves with false consolations: hooking up, alcohol, drugs, diet pills, eating disorders, cutting ourselves, and so on. All of this is done to cover up the wounds that aren't being healed."

Women caught in this cycle often feel hopeless and helpless. They may assume: "What's the point of hoping for love? Even if good men exist, why would they want a woman like me?" They feel so burdened and controlled by the past that they can't envision a better future.

Hundreds of women have confided in me about their personal stories of abuse, and one thing I always want them to understand is that I don't love my wife any less because of what happened to her. If anything, I want to love her *more*, to make up for what those other men did to her. Therefore, don't think you're worthless or worth any less because of your past. Don't be afraid that a good man wouldn't love you because of it. *If any good guy judges you by your past, then he's not that good a guy!* Hold out for a man who can see your future instead of settling for one who forever holds your past against you. Letting go of the past is hard enough without having someone in your life who never lets you forget it! You don't deserve that.

I mention this not because the goal of this book is to help you find love from a guy. It's not. Before you can do that, you face an even more important task: overcoming your fears and learning to love yourself. By this, I don't mean that you become infatuated with yourself and live fearlessly. It's okay to be afraid. The key is learning to fear the right things.

What a woman should fear is the possibility of determining her present value and future potential by the wounds from her past. You're more than the sum of your wounds. Although you may fear vulnerability, the greater danger is refusing to be vulnerable. When you lock up your heart, you may block the possibility of being hurt in some ways, but you also block the possibility of love. You may think that this is the only means by which you can protect yourself. But that's like thinking that the best way to avoid disappointment is to hope for nothing.

If your life is a book, the pages that have already been written might not look anything like you hoped they would. But the book isn't over. The rest of the pages are blank, and the pen is in your hand. Therefore, don't let go of hope, no matter how dark the past may be. If my wife abandoned hope, I don't think I would ever have met her. Our beautiful children would not exist. Because so much is at stake in your life as well, my wife and I wrote this book and have been praying for you— and praying that it would find its way into your hands.

—Jason Evert

Crystalina's Invitation

I don't know if you're a sexual abuse survivor, like me. Perhaps your story involves physical abuse, divorce, and infidelity, like mine does. Maybe you've suffered through an abortion or have wrestled with depression or stubborn, hidden addictions. I don't know your story, but what I do know is that you're not alone.

If you're like most women, you're tired of feeling like you're not enough. You feel like you're constantly failing or falling short of what you should do or who you could be. For many of us, this sense of inadequacy began in childhood. In my case, I learned from the earliest years that:

I was never good enough for my father to stay.
I was never valuable enough to be protected from sexual abuse.
I was never skinny enough for my boyfriends to be faithful.
I was never precious enough not to be hit.
I was never pure enough not to be labeled with degrading names.

If these lies are left unchecked, their effects can last a lifetime.

Years after these toxic relationships ended, I found a wonderful husband and began raising a family with him. But it wasn't long before the wounds of my past resurfaced. I felt that I wasn't whole enough to be the wife that I knew my husband deserved, or the mother that my children needed. I felt like a paralytic being expected to swim. While drowning in an ocean of my own inadequacies, I discovered that the betrayal came from within. The problem wasn't the demands of marriage or motherhood. The problem was that I had never untied the knots that bound me.

Perhaps you have been wounded by someone. Perhaps your wounds have been self-inflicted through your own choices. Regardless of who caused the hurt or when it happened, the past doesn't need to dictate your future or your identity.

All too often, instead of identifying our wounds, we identify ourselves by them. We live out of our wounds. Sometimes we act as if we're empowering ourselves through victimhood. In other words, we refuse to heal so that we'll never need to be accountable for the direction our lives are taking. We can always blame our bad choices on something or someone. But this isn't empowerment. It's surrender.

Ladies, it's time to banish whatever tempts us to despair and stands in the way of the life we've always wanted. At some point in life, we need to slay our insecurities so that they no longer control us. It's time to put the masks down and look at the ugly. Not only do we need to ditch the fronts we put on for others, hoping they'll think we have it all together, it's time to drop the masks we constantly show ourselves.

Because the healing process sometimes feels overwhelming or impossible, women are tempted never to begin. That's why we created this small book. I have learned that if you own your wounds, they will have less power over you. If you name the lies, you can take authority over them. But to do this, you need to show up to your own fight.

What follows are the twenty-five lies we tell ourselves in an effort to excuse ourselves from the effort required to be made new. We'll walk with you through each of the fears you may be facing, and defuse the power of the lies by speaking truth into each of them. One by one, we want to help untie the knots that exist in your life and show you that healing is possible, regardless of the past.

It's time to face it, to own it, and to heal it.

I'm fine. Really.

What lie do we tell ourselves more than this one? Odds are, you've never felt the need to look up the definition of "fine" in a dictionary. But here's what it says: "well or healthy: not sick or injured." When was the last time you felt this way? If we're honest with ourselves, it has probably been quite awhile. However, admitting this is much more difficult than hiding behind words like "fine."

We've all done it in our own way. Because we don't want to deal with a specific situation—or the memories of it—we escape. We run to something as simple as food and shopping or as serious as drugs, alcohol, or loveless relationships. In time, our temporary solutions become permanent crutches that we rely upon to cope with life. We cling to them because we want the pain of worthlessness and the feelings of inadequacy that haunt us to stop, even for a moment. In time, those false consolations become an addictive numbing medicine.

Because I didn't know how to handle the weight of the baggage from my past, these coping mechanisms became a vicious cycle for me. I hated being alone and going to bed at night because it seemed like the silence always screamed the truth. I felt lost, and the only solution I knew was to distract myself.

Meanwhile, my exterior disposition would fool just about anyone. My life felt like a show for others, and my smiles were nothing but a disguise. Yet this mask only deepened my sense of feeling unknown. I wanted to be loved for what was underneath it, but was too afraid to drop it.

I eventually realized why I was desperate to cling to the lie that I was "fine." I believed it was unacceptable *not* to be fine. You *had* to keep it together. You *can't* fall apart. After all, what will others think?

But here's the truth: You're not fine, neither am I, and that's okay. Let's get over this ridiculous expectation that our lives should look like a filtered social media photo. Instead of trying to mold our public image to fit a standard of bogus perfection, let's admit our brokenness and move forward to build a life that's truly fine.

It doesn't matter.

Some lies might be hard to see, but this one is not. Exactly what doesn't matter? Do you not matter? Does your dignity and self-worth not matter? Did what happened to you not matter? Although this might be difficult to do, go back in your memories to when your wounds were caused. As soon as it happened, was your first reaction, "Oh, that wasn't a big deal"? Odds are, you felt quite the opposite. But because you didn't know what to do with the fact that it mattered so much, you began telling yourself and others that it didn't matter.

I often talked myself out of the reality of what happened in order to convince myself of a tamer version of the truth. But the first step in the process of healing wounds is naming them and recognizing that they matter. Give yourself the permission to feel your feelings instead of stuffing them and thinking your strength is measured by your capacity to be numb and stoic.

What happened to us matters, and we know it. Because that reality scares us, we minimize, deflect, and deny. But this won't help. You matter, and because of this, what happened to you matters. In order to heal, we need not only to admit this, but to declare it!

I can deal with it.

After admitting that I wasn't fine and that my wounds mattered, I reached the point where I knew something needed to be done. But because my hurts were so deeply personal, I assumed the best route to solving them would be to handle everything myself.

The first step I took to "deal with it" was to isolate myself and shut out the world. But this only made me weaker. I felt like I was locked in a room with the devil, imprisoned in solitary confinement with nothing but negative thoughts and feelings of shame. My secrets took control of me and I became a hostage to myself.

When women feel this gnawing sense of aloneness, they sometimes escape into quasi relationships, getting lost in online chats and digital fantasies, assuming this will be safer. But such "relationships" only leave one feeling lonelier than ever, because it's like expecting affection from a ghost.

I knew isolation wouldn't work, so I got out. As St. Francis of Assisi remarked, "When the soul is troubled, lonely and darkened, then it turns easily to the outer comfort and to the empty enjoyments of this world."[1] In my aloneness, I turned to drugs, drinking, and men. But the worse the relationships became, the more I would smoke and drink. I also struggled with eating disorders in an effort to feel a sense of control. But I wasn't dealing with my hurt through all these forms of self-medication. I was only picking different poisons to veil my brokenness. Because withdrawal, dead-end relationships, and substance abuse only infected my wounds, I looked elsewhere.

I felt so much pent-up rage from the abuse that I had suffered from my father and boyfriends that I knew it needed an outlet. I started to channel my rage through kickboxing. This, at least, wasn't harmful. But no matter how hard I punched and kicked, I still wasn't dealing with it.

No matter what you've been through, you *can* deal with it, but here's the question: Are you? Or are you refusing to deal with it by hiding it? To deal with it, you need to reject isolation and every false consolation. After all you've been through, you deserve true consolation.

It was my fault.

After a sexual assault, the victim often rewinds the timeline of events that unfolded, imagining what she could have done differently to bring about a better outcome: "If only I didn't go to that party . . . If only I had stayed sober . . . If only I had listened to my family and stayed away from him . . . If only I had told someone instead of going back to him." As she considers the choices she made, she may begin blaming herself for the abuse.

What if she was dressed immodestly? Would that make it 2 percent her fault? How about if she was drunk and she said yes before she said no? Would that make it 10 percent her fault?

No! Abuse is always 100 percent the fault of the abuser. A woman's level of sobriety and modesty is not an indication of her willingness to be violated. Therefore, if you blame yourself for your abuse, stop. Even if a woman were unclothed and unconscious, a true man would guard her in her vulnerability rather than take advantage of it.

It's true that women can do certain things to decrease the likelihood of abuse, such as staying close to reliable friends, avoiding unsafe environments, not leaving their drink unattended, and so on. But even if every precaution is taken, abuse can still happen. And even if every precaution is overlooked, the blame does not belong to the victim.

Imagine how offended you would be if you heard a judge during a sexual abuse case blaming the victim of the abuse and ignoring the guilt of the aggressor. You'd fume! But here's the problem: Have you become such a judge to yourself? We've absorbed blame that is not ours, and have dealt ourselves additional unnecessary abuse through the shame we feel. If you find yourself doing this, please stop. It was not your fault.

I can't tell anyone.

Women often have strong reasons to keep secrets. If you've been betrayed, abused, raped, molested, or had an abortion, you may think, "No one can know. If I tell anyone, it will be a mess. They'll never look at me the same. It's not worth it." Such a woman may fear retaliation or looks of shame. She might want to cling to her disguise in order to maintain control of how she's viewed by others. If she was abused by someone within her family, she may fear the chaos that will ensue if the truth is revealed.

But despite all of these worries, not only *can* you tell someone what happened, you *must*. Your heart was never created to bear this burden alone, and your healing is far more important than anyone else's reputation.

Don't conceal the past out of fear that you'll be a burden to others. You don't need to hide the truth or apologize when you need help. While some women never want to say "sorry," others seem addicted to apologizing. But it isn't because they're truly apologetic. It's because they want to be reassured that they're not a burden. They assume, "No one wants to deal with me. Why would they?"

It's easy to understand why someone who has been deeply hurt by another might feel this way. If someone was careless with them, they'll doubt that they deserve care. As much as they pretend not to desire compassion, their refusal to reach out for it is in fact a cry for compassion! They want someone to break through their icy exterior.

If you find yourself doing this, stop. When we lack the courage and humility to seek help, we pretend as if our silent martyrdom is an act of consideration for other people's time and effort. It's not. When people you love are suffering, do you consider them a burden? In the same way, those who love you want to help you to feel alive again. But it's impossible for them to do this if you conceal your wounds. Let go of your fears and remember that feeling good again is more important than clinging to a good image.

If you fear that telling the truth will pose a risk to your personal safety, be prudent about whom you tell first. Make sure it's someone who can ensure that you have the necessary protections in place. You should never have to live in fear of doing the right thing. Besides, who knows how many others you might protect in the future by bringing the truth to light now?

When we keep our wounds locked away, our past will continue to haunt us. We'll feel a constant battle between who we've become and who we want to be. But this is a pivotal moment in your healing process. This is one battle that no one can fight on your behalf. Don't be intimidated. You're stronger than you think. If you need a little extra motivation, consider this: I used to believe that if I remained silent about my abuse, I was protecting myself. But my silence was only protecting my abuser.

At difficult moments such as this, don't hesitate to ask God for help. Pray for strength. He accepts you as you are. It doesn't matter how bad your situation may be, God is bigger than all of it. He is the only one who can undo what has been done, and through him alone can we find wholeness and deliverance.

No one will believe me.

When a woman shares her story of abuse and people in her family or in positions of authority say that they do not believe her, they're probably lying. Odds are, they do believe her, but they're too cowardly to do anything about it. So, they deny the allegations and blame the victim for causing drama and division, without pausing to ask why a woman would fabricate such a tale.

If this has happened to you, don't stop when you meet resistance. In 2018, dozens of female athletes received an award at the ESPYs for speaking out against their sexual abusers. But not one of them was awarded when they first spoke up. On the contrary, gymnast Aly Raisman testified:

1997, 1998, 1999, 2000, 2004, 2011, 2013, 2014, 2015, 2016. These were the years we spoke up about Larry Nassar's abuse. All those years, we were told, "You are wrong. You misunderstood. He's a doctor. It's OK. Don't worry. We've got it covered. Be careful. There are risks involved." The intention? To silence us in favor of money, medals, and reputation. But we persisted, and finally, someone listened and believed us. This past January, Judge Rosemarie Aquilina showed a profound level of understanding by giving us each an opportunity to face our abuser, to speak our truth, and feel heard. Thank you, Judge, for honoring our voices. For too long, we were ignored, and you helped us rediscover the power we each possess. You may never meet the hundreds of children you saved, but know they exist.[2]

Aly noted a crucial point about the importance of speaking up against abusers. Odds are, you are not their first victim, nor will you be their last if you remain silent. But if you can speak up, your courage has the potential to save countless other victims. Imagine all the young gymnasts who are now free to develop their talents without having their innocence threatened.

If you're being abused now, know that although some people might disbelieve you, others will believe. It is your task to find them. They might be a counselor at school or church, a teacher, a police officer, or a relative. Only you have the power to stop the situation and speak up. Don't be afraid of that power. Use it. Your voice is the key to your freedom. It opens the cage of secrecy that binds you. Only then can you move forward to receive the help and healing you deserve.

I don't need counseling.

No one wants to admit she's broken and needs a therapist. I used to think, "How embarrassing!" But there is no shame in wanting to be whole. However, coming to this realization can be a long journey.

My abuse began when I was a small child, and continued in different ways until I was eighteen. The self-destructive lifestyle I had chosen in order to deal with the hurt came to an end just before I went to college.

Although I never went to counseling, I changed my life and even became a missionary. I found my husband, started our family, and assumed that all of my baggage could be left outside the church as I entered this new phase of my life. I had finally arrived.

God had given me everything I wanted, and yet one day I found myself sobbing in the kitchen. I wasn't the wife I wanted to be, nor the mother. I was often angry and felt inadequate and incapable of giving and receiving love. One of the purposes of marriage is the sanctification of the spouses, but this means that our faults and wounds will come to the surface in order to be healed. Mine weren't gradually seeping to the surface; they were erupting.

As I was crying, Jason walked into the kitchen and knew what I was feeling. He wrapped his arms around me and said, "Don't worry, honey. You're just under construction." I had to laugh, because he was right. I knew it was time to find a good counselor and begin dealing with everything I had swept under the rug for more than a decade.

I once heard it said, "You're as sick as your secrets, and your secrets keep you sick." How do you know when it's time to get these secrets out? Here's a checklist of things to consider. The more of these items you recognize, the sooner you should find a good counselor:

- Difficulty sleeping
- Recurring nightmares
- Excessive fears
- Traumatic experiences in your past
- An inability to manage emotions in a healthy way
- A perceived need to hide the truth from others
- Significant fluctuations in your mood
- Depression or suicidal thoughts
- Destructive behavior
- A habit of negative self-talk
- Excessive anxiety
- Fear of aloneness
- Social isolation
- Fear of being alone with another
- Substance abuse or addictions
- Disruption in your performance at work or school
- A pattern of instability in your relationships with others

If you can relate to some of these things, take action. To find a good counselor, check out the list of websites at womenmadenew.com. However, you may need to shop around. If the first one doesn't quite fit, try another. Don't feel obligated to commit to one that doesn't seem right for you. Invest serious effort in this search and it will pay off. Find a counselor you connect with and dive in. When you find someone who feels trustworthy and safe, you will be able to make tremendous progress. The greatest gift you could give yourself is to dedicate yourself now to this healing process.

As you decide which counselor is right for you, here are questions worth asking before your first appointment:

- What is your training and experience?
- Have you treated many people with this issue?
- What treatment approaches do you use and how do they work?
- Is there a charge for the service? If there is, what is the fee and are there payment options?

Although this step may seem frightening, it often brings the quickest relief. If you have been burdened by shame, know that you can conquer it. Although the things that happened to me were shameful and I acted shamelessly afterward, I do not live in shame any longer, and neither should you. There is no shame in revealing what happened to you so that you can heal and become the woman you were created to be.

I'll get help later.

A friend in high school who was also in an abusive relationship told me I should try out the counselor she found. I knew I needed the help, but I thought therapy would be humiliating. I also thought of therapists as specialists who helped older people deal with mental problems. So, I figured I'd get help . . . later.

I felt some satisfaction in this. I believed I was actually doing something about my problems by making a commitment to deal with them later. In my mind, it would definitely happen, but now was not the ideal time. What began as a mere habit of postponement became an absolute talent. I had already perfected the art of keeping everyone out, so why would I want to ruin all that hard work and let someone in? My facade would crumble.

When you postpone your own healing, it's difficult to see the effects of the procrastination at first. But as the years go on and we see no noticeable improvement in our lives, we begin to wonder, "What portion of my life do I want to live as a mere portion of myself? What would it be like to feel whole again?" Allow that healthy curiosity to grow within you, because what you do today matters. After all, you don't have "later." That's why nothing has ever been accomplished later. You only have today.

When you don't seize the opportunity today, consider what may happen: I recently met a woman who had been molested by her father from childhood until she was eighteen years old. As soon as she could move out, she did. She knew she needed healing, but promised herself she would take care of it eventually. She wrote to me and said that she had postponed her healing for many years, and was now ready to face those memories and begin repairing the damage. She was seventy-five years old.

I can't deal with this.

At the age of seventeen, I found myself home alone, bawling on the kitchen floor. I felt worthless and suffocated under my sins and the sins of others against me. I wondered, "What would it be like just to be dead? It feels like that's what everyone wants. It would be better if I was gone. No one would miss me."

I grasped the crucifix around my neck in order to rip it off. I hesitated, knowing that if I took it off, I would do something horrible. I teetered on the edge of surrendering to the power of my wounds, as I felt them pulling me into a black hole. In the depth of my aloneness, I felt a voice within me telling me to stop. I unclenched the cross and began sobbing.

At every moment, we have a decision to move forward or back. It may not always be this dramatic, but it's no less important. When we say "I can't," we're trying to escape from the fact that what we really mean is "I won't." The question is never "can" versus "can't." It is always "will" versus "won't." Therefore, never underestimate your power to choose.

I'll never be healed.

When I began to realize the path of healing that was before me, I felt overwhelmed. The extent of the wounds seemed too intimidating to confront. At this point, despair began to set in—as well as a host of other emotions. I began to think of excuses for why I should discontinue counseling.

Moments of discouragement are bound to come during this process, so don't be surprised by this and give up on it. You may be tempted to think, "What's the point of exerting so much effort to reach a goal that I doubt exists? Why should I bother reviving awful memories, opening wounds, and compromising my privacy, when no one can change the past? The hurt will never go away."

While it's true that we cannot be the same person we were before our wounds were caused, we can become stronger than we were before. It has been said that suffering can make us bitter or it can make us better. The choice is ours.

In order to become better, we have to accept the fact that healing is a process. Like a physical wound, emotional healing takes time. Scar tissue may remain. But if we don't begin cleansing the wound, it can become infected and the damage can spread. Purifying wounds, whether physical or emotional, tends to be an uncomfortable process, but it's essential.

We can cleanse minor injuries ourselves, but the serious ones require more help. For these, it's helpful to remember that it's not your job to be the healer. In fact, the more serious a physical wound is, the more a patient needs to accept help from another to cure it. Anyone can put on a Band-Aid, but it takes a doctor to operate. Therefore, don't reach for a Band-Aid when you need surgery. Have the humility to receive help.

But remember that with any serious operation, the patient is likely to feel worse before she feels better. Don't be alarmed if you experience this, or assume that you're moving in the wrong direction. You're not. There's a purpose to your pain and there's a goal you're striving toward. The intensity of your struggle will not last forever. It's a season that will pass. To help you look beyond it, you may wish to come up with a list of the qualities you're working to possess. In my case, I wanted to be courageous, confident, and uncompromising. As you move forward, remember that hope is a choice, a gift, and a virtue. It's not a mood. You must choose it, ask God for it, and work to develop it.

I deserve the hurt.

One afternoon, while I was browsing through a menu of drinks on the countertop of a coffee shop, my eyes drifted up to the slender arms of the beautiful college-aged woman behind the counter. Her fair-skinned forearms were tattered with raised, pinkish scars, from cutting. Driving away that day, I could only imagine the story behind every one of those lacerations. Had she been wearing long sleeves, I would have assumed that her life was as pretty as her smile.

While some women inflict external wounds upon themselves to deal with their internal pain, I had the opposite problem. I assumed that I deserved to be hit and verbally abused by my boyfriend. I would think to myself: "I shouldn't have questioned him. It's my fault if he mistreats me. After all, I've done so many bad things in my own life, this is karma. I brought this on myself. It's not like I deserve something better. Some girls might deserve to be cherished, but not me. Not after all I've done. I deserve the hurt."

In essence, I had turned on myself. I hated myself for who I had become, and the wounds I allowed were an expression of my own self-loathing. I figured that it was the price I needed to pay. When we hurt ourselves or allow ourselves to be hurt, it is always an act of self-condemnation. It's false justice.

What we deserve is mercy, but we mistakenly think that needs to be earned. This is the root of the lie. Mercy cannot be earned. It is given. But you must choose to receive it. Whether your scars are internal, external, or both, you did not deserve them. Choose to see them in a new light. As one woman wrote to us, "My scars do still scare me sometimes, but I'm learning to see them as reminders of how far I've come rather than ghosts that haunt me."

I'll never be able to trust again.

After the traumatic experiences I had with men, I wanted to shield my heart. Deep levels of trust had been violated, and the individuals I thought would protect me did just the opposite. I knew from experience that if I gave my heart to any man again, I was bound to receive it back in pieces.

I began to equate relationships with hurt. In order to avoid further experiences of hurt and betrayal, I concluded that the most efficient path is to avoid close relationships—or to only pretend to be close. I became physically close to men, but my heart remained miles away from them. If I could keep everyone at arm's length, I'd be safe. The difficulty here is that what I wanted the most—love—required what I feared the most—vulnerability.

If you've ever felt the same, how do you break through this? Here are three essential steps.

First, renounce the vow you've made with yourself that you will "never" be able to trust again. That might be a strong feeling, but don't turn it into a decision. Instead, rephrase it: "I am afraid to trust anyone," "I don't know whom to trust," or "I don't know how to discern who is trustworthy." These are factual statements, and you'll make much more progress by tackling them individually instead of hiding behind some pledge to distrust everyone on the planet.

Second, accept the fact that although your trust has been violated—and perhaps many times—this does not mean that no one can be trusted. Early in life, a woman may tend to idealize the object of her affection. But after her trust has been violated, she may begin in future relationships to demonize the object of her affection. In other words, even if a man exhibits nothing but positive qualities, she will assume that, on a deeper level, something sinister is hiding within him, and it will only be a matter of time before his darker qualities emerge. This deep suspicion may cause her to feel afraid of being alone with any man.

The key is learning whom to trust, and when to trust them. Good men do exist, and when you find a man worthy of your heart, you won't have to protect your heart from him. He'll protect it for you.

Third, learn how to gauge a man's trustworthiness. Here's how:

- Take things slowly, and pace yourself in the friendship rather than getting too serious too fast. Enjoy the simplicity of a graced friendship. If he is as genuine as he seems, then he won't have a problem taking the time to build the necessary foundation of a lasting relationship.

- As you know, talk is cheap—especially when it's online. Therefore, make sure your friendship with this person is grounded in reality.

- Keep the friendship pure. If you are single, don't pretend that you're his girlfriend, because you're not. And if you're dating, don't behave like you're his bride, because you're not. When we get too close too soon, we lose our ability to judge rightly. Think of it this way: Try to read this book while holding it an inch away from your eyes. Give it a shot. How'd that work for you? In the same way, don't expect that you can objectively evaluate the quality of a man once you get in bed with him.

- Be honest with yourself about your attractions. Unfortunately, a woman's heart often doesn't care what her brain has to say. The brain could declare, "This guy is pretty much the total opposite of everything you want in a man," while the heart is replying, "Who cares if he's a convicted felon? He's super cute and I hope he likes me!" Sometimes we're more in love with the idea of a guy liking us than we are with the man himself. When we're starving for affection, it is easy to place an inflated and false value on the attention we receive from others.

- Don't go lone ranger. In other words, don't try to discern the quality of a man by yourself. Get frequent input from friends and family. They can often see what you cannot.

Ultimately, trust is more of a decision than a feeling. But it's a decision that requires prudence and wisdom. You might distrust your abilities to know whom to trust, but that can be developed. Give yourself the time to do this, because there's no need to rush into a relationship when you're in the midst of deep healing.

Love never lasts.

Growing up, I remember wrapping my arms around my grandfather and resting my head on his chest as we watched spooky movies together on his sofa. Since I never had a real relationship with my father, my grandfather filled a gaping hole in my life with his kind presence. Unfortunately, what little confidence I had in men was shattered when I learned at the age of eleven that he was cheating on my grandmother. I watched in sorrow as she sobbed uncontrollably when he walked out on her.

Growing up, I learned that divorce was inevitable. My parents divorced, and of my six aunts and uncles, five divorced. The scars of infidelity, addiction, and abuse could be seen on every branch of my family tree. I learned from these wounds that love never lasts, and only a fool would put her hope in it. Instead, a woman should build a wall around her heart and trust in no one but herself. She should be self-sufficient and remember that it's okay to give away your body, but whatever you do, don't give anyone your heart.

Little did I realize that while I was trying to liberate myself from the risk of betrayal and brokenness, I had become a prisoner of my own fears. The impenetrable walls I erected to protect my heart were only serving to keep people from loving me. I had not constructed a fortress for myself—I had built a jail.

By the time I met my husband, I had become so cynical and afraid of love that I immediately dismissed the possibility of him committing to me. I thought, "It won't happen, and if it does, it won't last. Don't give away your heart, because you'll pay the price for being dumb and naive enough to be vulnerable." As our friendship progressed, I realized that the emotional shield I was clinging to was also shielding me from joy.

I was faced with a decision: Do I allow the brokenness of my family tree to dictate my destiny, or do I create a different legacy? Do I prefer the predictability of feeling safe more than the chance of being loved? As I wrestled with this dilemma, I came to accept that no one could make this choice for me. The walls didn't crumble overnight, and in many ways I'm still working to dismantle them more than a decade into my marriage. But now I know that it isn't true that love never lasts. In fact, the only thing that lasts is love.

No one would want me.

While it's true that there are some people who do not want you (or will want you for the wrong reasons), this does not mean you lack value. Very few women ever realize this, but a woman's worth does not come from her level of desirability to men.

It was a sobering realization for me when I discovered that the men I had been dating didn't desire relationships—or me. They only desired the pleasure that came from having a relationship with me. I spent years mastering the ability to work this arrangement to my benefit—or so I thought. If I brought my contribution to the relationship (affection), they would provide theirs (attention). But this wasn't love. It was mutual use. Because I grew up feeling unwanted, my life became a perpetual quest to answer one question: What do I need to do in order to be cherished and desired? If it was degrading, then so be it. At least I would feel wanted for something!

When I ended those unhealthy relationships, it felt as if I was gradually emerging from a dense fog. I began to see that some people did love me, and I was the one who wasn't loving anyone. Therefore, take an assessment of your own life: Before you assume you're unloved, ask yourself, "How well am I loving others?"

Most single women wonder if they'll ever find love. They're troubled by the scarcity of good men in today's culture, and they feel the odds are against them when it comes to finding a decent one. Women who have suffered through sexual hurts in the past often share this concern, but they wrestle with an even deeper question: "Even if good men exist, why would such a man want a woman like me? If any guy knew the truth about me, he'd run. After all, why would someone accept me if I can't accept myself?"

As I mentioned above, when I met my husband, my first thought was that I could never have a guy like him. Pessimism had become part of my personality, and so my negative self-talk trampled any hopes as soon as they arose. Because safety was to be found only in solitude, hope was a dangerous thing. It posed a threat to my security. I was so accustomed to handling everything on my own that I developed the habit of isolation as a survival tool. Aloneness had become a choice. To open myself up to another meant uncertainty and risk.

But I figured, what's the alternative? Isn't it riskier to live in fear, and allow my phobia of rejection to drive me into isolation? That's not a risk worth taking. Although you might struggle to believe that you are wanted, here's the truth: You are wanted more than you will ever know in this life. Both heaven and hell want you, and will go to any extent to have you.

I'm damaged goods.

After being abducted and abused for nearly a decade, three women in Ohio escaped from the confines of their torturer. In their first public statement following the horrific experience, one of the women, Michelle Knight, stated, "I will not let the situation define who I am. I will define the situation. I don't want to be consumed by hatred."[3] With this bold profession, she not only renounced hatred toward her abuser, she also rejected his hatred for her. She refused to allow it to contaminate the way she viewed herself. Even after he had been jailed, she alone possessed the power to end the abuse.

Your future belongs to you, and there is no good reason why the hurts of the past need to dim the radiance of who you can become. You may feel useless, but you are important and no one can replicate the reason for which you have been created. No one can do the job that has been entrusted to you for the sake of humanity. You may scoff at such a grandiose thought, but God wanted you to exist for a reason. The scriptures promise, "For I know well the plans I have in mind for you, says the LORD, plans for your welfare, not for woe! plans to give you a future full of hope. When you call me, when you go to pray to me, I will listen to you. When you look for me, you will find me. Yes, when you seek me with all your heart, you will find me with you, says the LORD, and I will change your lot."[4]

Believe it or not, you can do something magnificent for the world. Therefore, never underestimate the power of your testimony and witness. If you think there's no need for your impact, imagine how many women are looking for hope in the eyes of another. As you progress in your own journey of healing, consider how many lives you can touch on the way. Realize the power of your voice not only to stop abusers, but to help victims of abuse to stop living out of their own wounds. You're not damaged goods! Like me, you may have suffered some "damage," but you are still good.

Depending upon what you have been through in life, some people might hold it against you. But don't worry about them. If someone is so obsessed with defining you by your past that they can't see who you have become today, then they don't deserve to be a part of your future.

I'm unlovable.

Because my history of abuse began during very early childhood, I internalized a crippling message: "You are deficient. If you *were* lovable, why would anyone have done to you the things that they did? In order to be loved in the future, you'll have to give something up. There will always be strings attached."

For many women, these wounds stem from their relationship (or lack thereof) with their father. One woman emailed us and recalled:

"When I was in second grade, I remember asking my dad if I looked pretty in my First Communion dress. I was too young to understand what alcohol was, so of course he was drunk when I asked him. His response to me was, 'Shut up, I'm not talking to you right now. I don't care about your stupid First Communion dress and how you look.' Being eight years old, all I could do was cry."

Without laying a hand upon her, he left a scar that lasted well into her adult years. When a young woman is abused or neglected by her father, she may gravitate toward similar relationships with men in her life. Such a dysfunctional relationship might make her feel connected to her own father. This indirect bond becomes more important to her than her own well-being. Meanwhile, living in harm's way feels more secure than remaining without such contact.

If a girl's needs are unmet by her parents, she may abandon the desire to fulfill those needs, because it's too painful to be constantly unsatisfied.[5] Instead of seeking true love, she may sexualize her problems and settle for lust. As strange as it sounds, promiscuity becomes a way for her to *escape* from intimacy. The thought of authentic closeness might trigger anxiety rooted in a fear of rejection or abandonment.[6] Thus, carefree sexual escapades offer her the illusion of closeness without having to give away her heart. But this never satisfies. As one woman said to us, "All of this left me drained and I felt like I had lost myself in this whirlpool of meaningless relationships."

How does one undo all this hurt and recover from it? Imagine a cup punctured repeatedly in its sides. No matter how much water is poured into it, it cannot be filled. This is like our hearts. The cup can only be filled once the holes are patched. When we take the time to reject our destructive thinking habits, heal from our hurts, and learn to love ourselves, we will be capable of receiving the love we deserve.

There's no point in saying no now.

After having been raped, a woman shared with us that she had discovered a way to ensure that it would never happen again: She would always say yes. The trauma that had been inflicted upon her when she tried to say no was so violating that she vowed never to utter that word again. That way, she could take control over any situation. Another woman wrote to us, "I just assumed that every guy only wanted to fool around and wouldn't stop until he got what he wanted, so I just gave him what he wanted. . . . Shockingly enough, every single one of the 'relationships' was short lived and the more physical they were, the faster they ended."

When a woman consents to abuse, it doesn't solve anything. It's like thinking you're winning a war by joining your enemy. You may feel that there's no point in offering any resistance in the future, but your dignity is worth fighting for. Don't give the final word to someone who failed to love you.

As Jason wrote in the foreword at the beginning of this book, there are so many blank pages waiting to be written in the story of your life. I know what it's like to fear that the stains of the past have tarnished even your future, but this doesn't need to happen. You may not have control over yesterday, but today and tomorrow are yours. As I once heard, "No matter how dirty your past is, your future is still spotless."

I can't change.

Have you ever noticed that bad habits are easily formed and difficult to break, while good ones are hard to form and easily broken? If you've noticed this pattern in your own life, you're not alone.

If you think lasting change is impossible because your efforts always seem to fall short, don't abandon your resolutions. Instead, take a deeper look at your approach. Perhaps you've been focusing too much on the fruit of the problem, rather than looking at the root of the problem.

For example, if your problem is that you're always trying to navigate through the drama of bad relationships, take a step back and ask yourself, "Could my lack of real intimacy with family, friends, and God be fueling my craving for false intimacy? Would the fleeting attention offered by insincere men seem so alluring if I satisfied my deeper needs?"

Looking at life this way requires more effort because we're inviting our intellect to chaperone our emotions. We're letting the head guide the heart. When the heart runs off on its own without supervision, it often leads us into messy situations. Sometimes we think of this as being spontaneous or romantic, but it's usually just being foolish. I say "we" because we've all done it. But what I noticed in my dealings with men is that when we get physical with one—especially when we're lonely—we begin filling in the gaps of his personality with the qualities we hope he has (but doesn't).

We also sometimes make the mistake of thinking that our vices are part of our personalities. For example, I used to believe that my anger and lack of self-control were simply part of "who I am." Because these traits had been a part of my personality for so long, I figured they were my temperament. The reality was that these flaws were rooted in unresolved hurts. Lasting change only took place within me when those hurts began to be addressed.

If you want to break a pattern of failed relationships, you need to be willing to make some major changes. Let's be honest: saying "I can't change" is an excuse. We don't lack the ability to change. We lack the motivation.

I can't leave him.

A young woman emailed us, saying, "I just want to feel like myself again, and not some pathetic person who degrades herself to please boys who don't care about me."

I know that feeling well. In my single years, I would sometimes dive into relationships so deeply that I began to experience the intimacy of a wife, the jealousy of a girlfriend, the compassion of a mother, and the concern of a sister. As you know, this is going too far. But when we invest that much into a relationship, it feels impossible to leave even when it's failing. It might feel like we're in a plane that ascended to an altitude of 30,000 feet . . . and then ran out of fuel . . . without a runway anywhere in sight.

If you've been questioning for a long time if your relationship is unhealthy, you have your answer. It's time for you step out of his shadow and live your life. It's time for *you*—and that's something that you probably didn't have much time for while you were with him. One day you will look back on this and wonder why you were so upset about leaving a situation that never made you happy to begin with.

The thought of being alone can be frightening, but we need to realize that the number one way to end up in a bad relationship is to allow the fear of loneliness to dictate our decisions. In high school, I remained in abusive, unfaithful, and impure relationships because it made me feel special (at times). Even though the guys mistreated me, I sought my self-worth and identity in them; I was somebody because I was with them. Without realizing it, I had made a god out of the relationships. Instead of finding my sense of meaning and worth in the God who loved me perfectly and would never leave me, I put imperfect men on the throne of my heart.

Despite all the problems in my relationships, I tried to ignore the reality of the situation and focus on the illusion, on what I hoped it could be. I could only ignore reality for so long. I knew in my heart that their wavering attention offered me nothing more than false acceptance.

God wanted more for me, and I knew it was time to begin wanting more for myself. It took a couple of failed attempts, but I finally broke free. As much as I yearned for a loving relationship at that time, I learned that many men aren't mature enough to provide it. They might not intend to break our hearts, but they certainly haven't learned how to cherish them.

But it isn't only the men who are sometimes unprepared for love. To the extent that we think we can't be alone, to that same extent we are unprepared to date. Indeed, we are not created to be alone. But we're not created for codependence either.

Breaking up might be frightening. You may feel trapped out of fear of what he will do to himself, to you, or to someone you love if you leave him. But it is not your job to be his mother or his messiah. Your job is to protect yourself and remove toxic relationships and people from your life. If it looks like the breakup will be messy, don't attempt to do it on your own. Find someone who can help you to make this transition safely. But not only *can* you leave him, you *must*.

Perhaps your unhealthy relationship isn't with a boyfriend. Perhaps he's your husband. What are you to do? You promised to remain true to him in good times and bad. Each situation is different, but one promise you never made to him was that you'd be willing to be abused. That wasn't part of the wedding vows. Therefore, don't feel guilty about seeking counseling to discern whether you need to separate for your safety, or if you can restore the marriage through couples and individual counseling.

I can't forgive.

Maria was an eleven-year-old girl who had no choice but move in with another family after her father passed away, due to her poverty. When the twenty-two-year-old son of the other family attempted to seduce her, she rejected his advances. In a fit of rage, Alessandro attempted to choke her, and then stabbed her fourteen times. The next day, as she was dying in her hospital bed, she forgave him.

Years later, as he slept alone a prison cell, she appeared to him in a dream, offering him fourteen lilies representing forgiveness for the fourteen times he wounded her. When he awoke, Alessandro reformed his life, and upon his release from prison many years later, stood among the crowd of believers who gathered in the Vatican as Maria Goretti was declared a canonized saint.

Such a dramatic story might seem inspiring but unattainable. In my story, forgiveness was not my first step in the healing process. If anything, it was the last. When others wound us, our natural inclination is to cling to bitterness, hatred, and resentment. When people tell us "forgive and forget," it feels as if they're asking us to prove our forgiveness by having amnesia. This isn't helpful.

What we need to realize is that forgiveness is not a feeling. It's a choice. It's a decision to wish mercy upon another instead of harm. Forgiving someone does not mean that the person shouldn't be brought to justice. He or she should. But it also means that we let go of our craving for vengeance and retaliation. We might be tempted to wish harm on the person who harmed us, but by refusing to forgive, we do not bring any harm to the other; we only punish ourselves. If you feel incapable of forgiving others, pray for the gift of a merciful heart and remember that forgiveness is not a sign that the offense was unimportant. It's a sign that mercy is powerful, and that love is stronger than hate.

Forgiveness often requires heroic virtue—especially when the person we need to forgive is ourselves. In my case, this took more time and effort than forgiving my abusers. It's one thing to be abused by another person, but it's an entirely different battle when you internalize the abuse and begin doing it to yourself.

I became a master of negative self-talk as a form of self-punishment. I would say to myself: "Crystalina, how did you let this happen? You asked for it. You knew better, or at least you should have known better. You brought it on. You could have stopped it, but you didn't. You should be ashamed." I even became addicted to echoing the verbal abuse I had heard. I would think to myself: "I'm so fat. I'm so stupid. I'm a slut."

As these insults, doubts, and lies fester and become habitual, they mature into the "never" and "always" statements that we feed ourselves. For example: "You'll *never* change, or trust, or heal." Or: "You'll *always* be disappointed or a failure." We unknowingly make vows to ourselves, setting ourselves up for failure. We become blind to the goodness we possess.

It's time to break those vows and habits. Yes, you might feel anger toward yourself for certain choices you have made, but stop beating yourself up. Where has that gotten you, anyway? You don't have to admire everything in your past, but you can learn from it. Take those hurts and use them as fuel that will propel you to never again return to that lifestyle. If you've made some mistakes, forgive yourself for them. Be merciful to yourself, as you would be toward anyone else who had been through the same things in life.

God abandoned me.

What if an innocent girl was stripped naked in front of her peers, beaten, and then murdered? Would you consider that to be sexual abuse? Absolutely! What if men did all of this to her but they technically never touched her in a sexual way while humiliating her. It's still sexual abuse, right?

What if the victim wasn't a young girl, but a grown woman in a foreign land who was charged with crimes she never committed? Would it be less of an offense to publicly shame her in this manner? What if this all happened centuries ago, long before the Me Too movement? Would it still be wrong?

What if it happened to a little boy? Again, sexual abuse is sexual abuse. The gender and age of the victim is irrelevant.

Let's change one more detail in the narrative: What if it happened to a man who lived two thousand years ago in Jerusalem?

It did.

As scandalous as this may be to read, we worship a sexually abused God.

We have a savior who took on our humanity in order to take on our shame. We have a God who knows the pain of betrayal, abandonment, humiliation, and violence, who shows us that not only can wounds be healed—they can also be glorified.

As alone as you may feel at times, your tears are not unseen by God. The Bible says that God has kept our tears in a bottle.[7] Not only has he witnessed our sorrow and shared in it, he promises that he "will wipe away every tear from their eyes . . . neither shall there be mourning nor crying nor pain any more, for the former things have passed away."[8]

Don't be afraid to hope in these promises. After all, hope is not merely an optimistic feeling. It's a virtue. It's not something that comes from within, by the power of positive thinking or the latest self-help techniques. Hope comes from God, and it's something we need to ask for.

You may question God because of things that have happened to you, and wonder where he was when you needed him the most. This is understandable. You may ask yourself: "If God is all-good, all-knowing, and all-powerful, why didn't he intervene?" Was he not powerful enough? Did he not know? Or did he not care enough to prevent it from happening?

What you might not realize is that these questions are prayers in themselves. The book of Psalms is filled with prayers that cry out, "My God, my God, why have you abandoned me? Why so far from my call for help, from my cries of anguish? My God, I call by day, but you do not answer; by night, but I have no relief . . . Because of you my acquaintances shun me; you make me loathsome to them; Caged in, I cannot escape . . . my only friend is darkness."[9] What we can learn from this is that God is not dishonored when we express to him our anguish and frustrations. He's listening, and he has answers to give if we're willing to listen as well.

If you have been running from God, stop for a moment. Invite him into those memories and places in your life where you need healing the most. Watch what can happen. He is faithful, and will not forsake you. Entrust not only the past to him, but also your future.

If you feel that God has abandoned you, don't let go of hope. If you're being called to marriage and motherhood one day, then generations of people yet to be born depend upon your courage to hope. Think about it: When you choose which men you will date, you are potentially choosing a father and grandfather of your future family. The gravity of such a choice may feel intimidating, but don't worry about tomorrow. All we have is today, and God is with you today.

God won't forgive me.

Although it's never a sin to be abused, when others fail to guard our innocence, we sometimes follow their lead. If others are reckless toward us, it's easy to become reckless with ourselves. I assumed, "Once it's gone, it's gone. What's the point of practicing chastity?"

After wasting so much time in darkness, buried under the weight of years of shame and embarrassment, I yearned for forgiveness but never felt worthy to receive it. I figured that once I turned my life around and began living like a real Christian, then and only then would he look kindly upon me. In the meantime, my sins were too big, and there were too many of them. In my mind, he would love me only when I'm perfect, but it was too late for that.

Sometimes I would go to the sacrament of confession in order to appease my mother, but I wouldn't take it seriously. I considered it to be nothing more than an optional humiliation ritual. I'd even make up sins, keep the big ones to myself, and walk out as if I hadn't just committed sacrilege. Years later, I began to understand that confession isn't God's way of placing a hurdle between himself and us. Rather, he's showing us how near he wants to be to us in our brokenness.

Therefore, find a good priest, and consistently go to him for confession. It is humbling when you confess the same kinds of sins month after month. But this increases in us the virtue of humility, and helps the priest to provide better spiritual direction. If we hide our wound from the physician, it cannot heal.

Although I once dreaded going to confession, it gradually became for me a source of joy. I discovered unique gifts of healing that I found nowhere else. Not only did confession take away the guilt of my sins, it also provided me graces to avoid those sins in the future and reassured me that God is with me in the mess.

It's okay if your past is messy. Sometimes the process of healing is messy as well. Just look at the Gospels! Jesus sometimes used mud and spit to cure the deaf, mute, and blind![10] Perhaps he wanted to communicate to us that he's not afraid of the mess. The devil often tries to convince us that we are unworthy, but one writer noted we should "laugh at the absurdity of the situation: Satan, the epitome of sin itself, accuses *you* of unworthiness! . . . When the devil reminds you of your past, remind him of his future!"[11]

God can't take away the past.

You're right. Although God can't take away the past, he can prevent the devil from robbing you of your future. For years, I let this happen. I would give God my sins, but then I'd hold on to the hurt, blame, and shame, not realizing that he wanted to take these away too.

I never seemed to make much spiritual progress during that time of my life, because so many of my vices were rooted in my unhealed wounds. It was as if the devil had the authority and permission to oppress me because I hadn't shut those doors on him.

Because I grew up watching horror movies, I developed an unrealistic idea of the demonic world. I assumed the devil was nothing more than the product of Hollywood's special effects. Or he was just a fictitious character—the result of people's overactive imaginations or mental problems. I am now quite certain that he is pleased when people dismiss him in this manner. That way, he can work more freely and effectively in the world, as we gradually offer him access into our lives through our subtle compromises.

One way we do this is by refusing to allow God into our wounds to heal them. Sometimes emotional wounds prevent spiritual progress, and sometimes unconfessed sins prevent emotional growth. In order to be made new, we need to seek healing for our hearts and minds as well as our souls. By doing this, we block the devil's ability to afflict us in countless ways because he cannot follow us into the light.

Therefore, do not be afraid of the evil you may have encountered. As the scriptures instruct, "Resist the devil and he will flee from you."[12] Remember that although the past cannot be changed, it can always be redeemed.

God can't love me.

Perhaps because I never had a father who showed me unconditional love, I always had a tainted view of God. If something bad happened to me, I assumed that God must be punishing me. I didn't realize that he had already paid the price for my sins. I figured that I needed to atone for the past, and these sufferings must be God's way of enacting his justice on me.

One night, all of this began to change. As I was driving past a church late at night after a party, I felt an unexpected urge to pull over. Sitting in the parking lot, I pondered if I should actually go into the Adoration chapel. Based upon what I had been doing at the party one hour earlier, I felt like I had no business being there. I always figured that God has his favorites, and I was obviously not one of them.

Yet, something was tugging at me. Perhaps it was God calling me toward him, or maybe it was just the fact that my lifestyle left me feeling so dissatisfied and hollow. Looking back, now I see that it was both.

So, I decided that if I had tried everything else in high school, I might as well try God. I walked into the chapel and knelt before the Blessed Sacrament. There was no flash of lightning or voice from heaven. Actually, I was thinking about the elderly lady sitting in the corner, wondering if she could smell the aroma of pot on me. There was pure silence. I was alone with him.

At this time in my life, I struggled with relating to Jesus as a man, because of how many times I had been hurt by men. But because his Presence was veiled in the Eucharist, I was able to approach him without this obstacle between us.

At first, it was hard to look up at the Eucharist. I just buried my face in my hands, and debated if I should just leave. I didn't feel like reciting memorized prayers. So, I just raised my eyes and said, "God, here I am . . . in my filth. Please help me." I felt torn between the life I had known for years and a God I hardly knew. His invitation was clear, but my future seemed so uncertain. All he was saying to me was: "Let go and trust me."

From that moment, I understood that God does not only want my goodness. He wants the ugly. He doesn't like sin, to be sure, but in order for him to embrace me and have a relationship with me, he wanted to embrace me exactly as I was, even with all of my faults. That's the start of an authentic relationship with God.

Because I thought that I needed to become a saint in order for him to love me, I always kept him at a distance. But it is precisely when you feel most torn between God and sin that you need to be still and let him love you. Only when you understand your value in his eyes will you be able to change. You won't be motivated by shame, guilt, or fear, but because you know you deserve love. Knowing his love for you will give you the motivation to love yourself. And if you struggle to forgive yourself, it helps to know that he has already forgiven you.

When you know you are loved by someone, you trust them. The same is true with our relationship with God. When we trust him, we begin to practice what is perhaps the most powerful virtue in the world: obedience. This word is often viewed in a negative way and equated with submission. But in reality, it is the key that unlocks a vault of limitless graces. When we turn away from the will of God, we block off so much goodness that he wishes to give to us.

At every time in my life when I had a choice between good and evil, I would hear in the depths of my soul a voice reminding me what was right. I can't say that I always heeded that voice. But I can say that I never regretted listening to it, and always regretted ignoring it. Although choosing the good might seem difficult, know that God will never fail to give you everything you need to make that choice. It is always within your reach. Besides, when we don't choose the good, don't our lives become even more difficult?

Even in the darkest hours of my life, I knew God was within reach. No matter how far I ran from him, I knew he was waiting. I endlessly tried to silence this sense of his presence, but could not. Don't exhaust yourself fleeing from his love, because it isn't going anywhere.

Regardless of your past, you don't need to earn God's love. You just need to accept it. No matter what you have been led to believe, you are lovable. It does not matter where you've been or what you've done. All that matters now is where you go from here.

God can't use me.

Margaret ran away from her parents' home in Italy at the age of seventeen and began living with her boyfriend. He promised to marry her, but the day never came. She wanted to do something great with her life, but she remained in her unhappy relationship. After having a child with her boyfriend and cohabiting with him for ten years, he was murdered while on a journey. After his death, Margaret attempted to move home with her father and stepmother, but the wife refused.

Alone and homeless with her child, she prayed for direction and she seemed to hear a voice within her soul urging her to go to the Franciscan Friars in Cortona, Italy. She followed this prompting, and spent the rest of her life there serving the sick and poor, and growing in holiness. She established a congregation of sisters, built a hospital, and was canonized a saint in 1728! Today, her body lies incorrupt in a magnificent Italian church, dedicated in her name. It's reassuring to know that a woman who lived with her boyfriend and had a child out of wedlock is now honored as a saint!

If you study the lives of the saints, you will quickly discover that sainthood is not about being put into a mold. Each saint is intensely unique. Some had fiery temperaments, like St. Catherine of Siena. Others, such as St. Gemma, were known for their deep mystical life. Some gave their lives to serve orphaned children, while others became scholarly nuns or doctors who were also holy wives and mothers. Some lived in a convent since their youth, while others escaped from a life of prostitution or slavery.

No matter your personality or your past, God has a plan for you. Do not be afraid to become yourself and do something remarkable for the world! You have a testimony and gifts that God has given to no other. Do not underestimate these treasures, because you never know whose darkness your light alone can pierce.

However, God isn't the only one with a plan for your life. The devil has one too. His plan is simple enough: he wants you to live in fear. In fact, the greatest weapon that hell uses against women is fear. I think this is because hell fears women. The source of all beauty is God, and nothing on earth compares to the beauty of women. Because you are a reflection of heaven, you're the most alluring being on earth. It's who God made you to be. Every woman has the power to lure mankind to heaven or to hell. She is a walking, breathing, invitation to eternity—in either direction. Unfortunately, the world wants you to trade in your power to allure for the mere capacity to seduce. Instead of teaching you how to reveal your worth, it encourages you to expose yourself.

Instead of blooming into the person God created you to be, the devil wants you to forfeit your dignity and then hide in fear under a mask. If you've been living in such a disguise, stop being afraid of what's beneath it. What you ought to fear is the mask itself, because it covers up who you truly are. You are not some tangled mess of wounds, although it may sometimes feel like that. That is not your identity. You are a beloved daughter of God the Father, and that's who you are.

No matter what your future may be, now is not meant to be a time of waiting. God is teaching you something each step along the way, and is preparing you for more than you can imagine. Take his hand, and walk with him, trusting that he is never outdone in generosity.

If you're unsure how to begin the process of healing, here are the four pillars that supported my entire restoration process:

First, find a great counselor and be transparent about everything you've experienced.

Second, find a good priest to whom you can be accountable, in order to receive confession and spiritual direction.

Third, spend time in Eucharistic Adoration, especially after your counseling sessions, taking time to process through prayer and journaling what you learned. This has transformed me as a woman.

Fourth, remove toxic people from your life and replace them with those who will surround you with support and love.

I found that by doing these four things with consistency, I made more progress in a short span of time than I had in years of attempting all sorts of other solutions.

You have a light to show and a powerful love to offer. Don't be afraid that your scars will obscure the light. You might feel as if your life has been irreparably shattered, but consider this: When you bring shards of broken glass together and shine radiant light through them, you create stained glass. Likewise, God can bring beauty through our scars. He can turn us into living cathedrals. All we need to do is trust in his promise: "Behold, I make all things new."[13]

Endnotes

1   St. Francis of Assisi, as quoted in Johannes Jörgensen, *Saint Francis of Assisi: A Biography,* trans. T. O'Conor Sloane (New York: Longmans, Green, and Co., 1912), 289.

2   Aly Raisman, speech at ESPYs, July 18, 2018.

3   "Ohio Kidnap Victims Break Silence to Say 'Thank You,'" Doug Stanglin and Laura Petrecca, *USA Today,* July 9, 2013.

4   Jer 29:11–14 (NAB).

5   Cf. Christian Gostecnik, *Journal of Religion and Health* 46:4 (December 2007), 586.

6   Ibid., 589.

7   Cf. Ps 56:8.

8   Rev 21:4.

9   Ps 22:1–2; 88:9, 19 (NAB).

10 Cf. Mark 7:33, 8:23; John 9:6.

11 Fr. Joseph M. Esper, *Saintly Solutions to Life's Common Problems* (Manchester, NH: Sophia Institute Press, 2001), 182.

12 James 4:7.

13 Rev 21:5.

THE SEXUAL CULTURE WAR IS ON

SEXTING, FACEBOOK GOSSIP, PORNOGRAPHY, HOOKING UP, BROKEN FAMILIES, AND BROKEN HEARTS.

HOW DO YOU TURN PEER PRESSURE INTO PURE PRESSURE?

Jason and Crystalina Evert have spoken to more than one million teens on five continents. Now, schedule a presentation to have them inspire the youth in your junior high, high school, university, church, or conference.

Teens today need straight answers to tough questions about dating, relationships, and sexual purity. That's why Chastity Project offers more than a dozen presentations designed to empower students and parents.

FOR MORE INFORMATION, VISIT

CHASTITY.COM

GOT QUESTIONS? GET ANSWERS.

WATCH VIDEOS
GET RELATIONSHIP ADVICE
LAUNCH A PROJECT
READ ANSWERS TO TOUGH QUESTIONS
FIND HELP TO HEAL FROM THE PAST
LISTEN TO POWERFUL TESTIMONIES
SHOP FOR GREAT RESOURCES
SCHEDULE A SPEAKER

FOR $3 OR LESS, WHO WOULD YOU GIVE THESE BOOKS AND CDS TO?

In order to reach as many people as possible, more than 40 chastity CDs and books are available in bulk orders for $3 or less! Therefore, share this book and others like it with the people in your life who need it right now. For example:

YOUR COLLEGE DORM | YOUR HIGH SCHOOL
YOUR YOUTH OR YOUNG ADULT GROUP AT CHURCH | YOUR ALMA MATER

Buy a case of books and donate them as gifts at graduation, freshman orientation, retreats, conferences, confirmation, as a missionary effort through campus ministry, or to people you meet anywhere. You never know whose life you could change.

TO ORDER, VISIT